A Slight Misunderstanding

A Light Comedy

Adrian Dale

Samuel French—London
NewYork – Sydney – Toronto – Hollywood

Copyright © 19780 by Samuel French Ltd
All Rights Reserved

A SLIGHT MISUNDERSTANDING is fully protected under the copyright laws of the British Commonwealth, including Canada, the United States of America, and all other countries of the Copyright Union. All rights, including professional and amateur stage productions, recitation, lecturing, public reading, motion picture, radio broadcasting, television and the rights of translation into foreign languages are strictly reserved.

ISBN 978-0-573-13308-4

www.concordtheatricals.co.uk
www.concordtheatricals.com

FOR AMATEUR PRODUCTION ENQUIRIES

UNITED KINGDOM AND WORLD EXCLUDING NORTH AMERICA
licensing@concordtheatricals.co.uk
020-7054-7200

Each title is subject to availability from Concord Theatricals, depending upon country of performance.

CAUTION: Professional and amateur producers are hereby warned that *A SLIGHT MISUNDERSTANING* is subject to a licensing fee. Publication of this play does not imply availability for performance. Both amateurs and professionals considering a production are strongly advised to apply to the appropriate agent before starting rehearsals, advertising, or booking a theatre. A licensing fee must be paid whether the title is presented for charity or gain and whether or not admission is charged.

The Professional Rights in this play are controlled by Samuel French Ltd (Concord Theatricals), Aldwych House, 71–91 Aldwych, London WC2B 4HN.

This work is published by Samuel French, an imprint of Concord Theatricals.

No one shall make any changes in this title for the purpose of production. No part of this book may be reproduced, stored in a retrieval system, or transmitted in any form, by any means, now known or yet to be invented, including mechanical, electronic, photocopying, recording, videotaping, or otherwise, without the prior written permission of the publisher. No one shall upload this title, or part of this title, to any social media websites.

The right of Adrian Dale to be identified as author of this work has been asserted in accordance with Section 77 of the Copyright, Designs and Patents Act 1988.

CHARACTERS

Audrey
Carrie
Irma
Effie
Joyce
Lettice

The action takes place on a bare stage, where the audience "joins" a local women's guild for an afternoon meeting

Time—the present

NOTES

The play has no scenery and is simple enough to put on. Yet it makes demands. It needs to go at a good pace. The physical and speech differences of the characters need heightening. The timing of the series of opening entrances and exits is critical. Lettice's make-up and manner, although startling, should somehow be just about believable. Also there is considerable scope for inventiveness with the properties and "business", particularly in the four demonstrations.

If Joyce can rattle off with aplomb the list of things from which wine can be made, it is sure to be appreciated.

Audrey is an "ordinary" member of the audience who just happens to be dragged into the action. She has to be natural no matter how zany they are on stage. This is important for continuity and in making the audience participation effective.

A SLIGHT MISUNDERSTANDING

The CURTAINS *are open. The houselights dim and the stage lighting intensifies. The stage is bare except for a plain trestle table and a pile of five stacking chairs*

Audrey sits at the side of the front row, with the audience. Somehow, from where she is, she becomes naturally involved with events on stage

Carrie, a larger-than-life cheerful character, very direct, hurries in from the front of house through the audience towards the stage. She is loaded with a great heap of clothes, some books, toys, shoes, an umbrella and a bowler hat

Carrie (*as she walks along*) You lot are in good time, aren't you? I shan't be starting up my jumble for half an hour yet. That's the time we fixed for it, you know. We have to be fair to those that aren't here but will be coming. So I hope you don't mind waiting. Just so long as the stuff all sells, I don't mind. Hello, Audrey, I didn't see you at first.
Audrey Hello, Carrie. What's all this about a jumble? It's news to me.
Carrie What are you doing here then?
Audrey I thought we were here to watch some play or other.
Carrie Ah, get along with you. You're pulling my leg. (*She climbs up on the stage*) What about the bowler hat and brolly for your old man? (*She dumps her load on the table and spreads it out*) He'd be the best-dressed gravedigger in the country. (*She retraces her steps down through the audience*) Now I'm just going to get another load. It's only what I call a mini-jumble, Audrey. We're raising money for the old folks. But don't any of you worry about it. I'm strong. I can manage all on my own. You take it easy. Sit there in comfort and I'll do the work.

Carrie goes

Audrey (*to those round her*) Don't take any notice of her. She's always like that. Didn't you think you were here to see a play?

Lettice, who appears to have been waiting for Carrie to leave, nips on with a great bundle of teazles, branches of leaves and pampas grass. She has an extraordinary appearance—a long pointed nose, heavy make-up and large glasses. She wears a large cloche hat, with dried flowers on it, pulled right down over her head, and the clothes to match. She pushes the jumble aside to make room for her things; then she clears most of the remaining jumble on to the floor

Lettice Rubbish, rubbish.
Audrey Who on earth are you?

Lettice takes no notice, and spreads out her material

I say, what are you doing?
Lettice Oh! Are you addressing me actually?
Audrey Yes, you. I don't know your name.
Lettice Oh, call me Lettice. Short for Letitia.
Audrey No, thank you, I'd rather not. I think you should know that jumble was only just put there by someone. You're asking for trouble. She's a tough character when roused. She used to be a chucker-out for ladies-only bingo.
Lettice I am not perturbed. I am here by official invitation.
Audrey Well, I've warned you. I wouldn't like to be in your place when Carrie gets back.
Lettice We shall see. I have to fetch some more items myself. I shan't be long.

Lettice goes the way she came. Effie comes on from the other side of the stage. She is an untidy, eccentric person, rather jumpy. She carries a heavy tray of cooking ingredients

Effie In your usual place, Audrey, I see. Who was that with the hat?
Audrey For a moment I thought that must be the beginning of the play but that was Lettice.
Effie Lettice! I don't know any Lettice. What's she doing putting her garden rubbish all over my table? (*She rests her tray on the end of the table and pushes. The remainder of the jumble goes off the other end*)
Audrey Your table?
Effie What play? And what's all that old clobber doing on the floor?

A Slight Misunderstanding 3

Audrey What are *you* doing here, Effie?
Effie Don't you know? Are you serious? Hasn't it been announced? Oh. For those of you who do not realize, I shall be giving my talk and demonstration on unusual cookery.
Audrey Who did know about it, except you?
Effie Hetty of course. Where is she?
Audrey I haven't seen her.
Effie I can't help that. It's in about twenty minutes or so. If everyone's here I could begin sooner. First I've got some more things to collect.

Effie starts to go, almost colliding with Irma coming on. Irma appears to be thoroughly miserable and humourless. She carries a large cardboard box with her lampshade-making things in it

Irma Effie!
Effie Irma!

Effie goes

Irma goes to the table and pushes things aside to make space for her box. Some of Lettice's material falls off

Irma She was a little premature, wasn't she, Audrey? Does she think she's doing her talk this afternoon?
Audrey Yes, I believe she does. I suppose you think you're doing yours?
Irma Of course. Hetty arranged it. (*With enormous lack of enthusiasm*) This is my chance to shine.
Audrey What's your subject?
Irma You don't know? Oh dear. How to make lampshades that are different.

Joyce marches on stage from the same side as Irma. She is a confident, authoritative sort. She carries a large box of wine-making paraphernalia

Joyce Oh, people. Things. I saw Effie. Oh, hello, everybody! Irma! What are you doing here?
Irma What d'you think you're doing here?
Joyce I beg your pardon. I don't care for your tone of voice. If you must know, I'm preparing for my talk about home-made wine. It's in twenty minutes.
Irma That's all right by me if you do it somewhere else.

Joyce Whose cookery whatnots are these?
Irma Effie's.
Joyce If I move them there'll be room on the table for this first lot of mine. I suppose you wouldn't like to . . . No, I suppose you wouldn't. (*She puts down her box, moves Effie's tray to the floor in front of the table, then puts her box on the table*)
Irma Have you seen Hetty?
Joyce No. I don't need to. It's all arranged as far as I'm concerned. Isn't there a mess here? I do think people ought to clear up after their frolics. Now look, Irma, I'm going for my wine samples quickly and then we'll get to the bottom of this kerfuffle. You're staying right there, are you?
Irma I certainly am.
Joyce Good. Then don't let anyone move my bits and pieces. I'll be right back. (*She starts to go*) Good afternoon, Audrey.

Effie returns with more ingredients and utensils for cookery, almost colliding with Joyce

Effie Joyce!
Joyce Correct first time. And don't you dare move my things before I get back.

Joyce hurries off

Effie comes up to the table and stands there pathetically, not knowing what to do with her tray

Effie What's happening? You look as if you're waiting for a bus in a blizzard. What are *my* things doing on the floor?
Irma I don't know, but I think Joyce will become violent if her own stuff is moved.
Effie Did she put my tray on the floor? What shall I do with this one?
Irma Oh, it is all too much to bear. What about me—my lampshades—my talk—my sleepless nights wondering what to say?
Effie You don't have to do it, do you?
Irma Oh yes, I feel committed.
Effie It sounds as if you soon will be. I think I'll put this tray safely out of the way *under* the table. Then the other one as well perhaps.

Effie starts to put the tray she has just brought under the table

A Slight Misunderstanding

Carrie comes in from the front of the house, singing loudly. She has a huge pile of jumble in her arms and cannot see where she is going

Effie is so startled she hits her head under the table—and remains there, rubbing the bump

Carrie Here we are again, folks! Happy as can be! Won't be long now. Get your little handbaggies and purses at the ready. (*She swerves towards and away from the audience*) Whoops! Sorry, dear. Can't see where I'm going with this lot. There's quite a nice jacket that would suit you, Audrey. (*She continues singing as she makes her way up on stage*)

Effie Stop her, Irma, stop her! (*She tries to stand up and bumps her head again*)

Irma Carrie! Mind out! Look where you're . . .

Audrey Carrie!

Carrie Ah! (*She comes to a sudden stop with one foot firmly planted in Effie's aspic. After a while she holds up the load so she can look down. She lifts her foot and looks at it*) As I was saying—ah!

Effie (*still under the table*) My aspic—I'm ruined . . .

Carrie (*throwing down her load on top of the other jumble*) You might well have been if I'd trodden on you. What are you doing there? Where's Hetty? Who put my stuff on the floor? (*She begins to snort with fury. She looks round for something to destroy. She looks in Irma's box and grabs a couple of luridly coloured string lampshades*) What the heck are these?

Irma No, Carrie, no! They're my lampshades that are different.

Carrie Different! I'll say they're different. They're stupid, stupid!

(*She throws them down and jumps on them until they are permanently flat*)

Irma Murder! Murder! How could you? (*She runs to the spot, holds them up for all to see and bursts into tears*)

Carrie Well, I'm sorry, Irma, although I don't think I am really. I feel a bit better if anything.

Joyce hurries in with a tray of bottles, all different sizes, colours and shapes

Joyce Who's been murdered? What on earth is happening?

Irma Look! My precious objects ... Carrie did it.
Carrie I also put my foot in Effie's aspic but I'm damned if that was my fault.
Effie No, it was yours, Joyce. You put my tray on the floor. You're just a great bossy twit! On the committee! You shouldn't be put in charge of a Bath bun.
Joyce What are you doing under there? Come out at once.
Effie (*coming out, rubbing her head*) I meant it, every word of it. I'm not going to apologize. (*She gets a chair and sinks down on it*)
Joyce Now just a moment while I put this down. Then we'll sort everything out. (*She rests her tray on the end of the table and pushes. More things go off the other end*)
Carrie Look here, Joyce, I am just having a quiet little jumble and all of you bring things that are not really suitable. Homemade wine? Perhaps that'll go. But I don't think it's legal to sell it. Balls of string? Twigs. Cookery. It doesn't make sense.

Everyone begins to protest at once

Lettice enters from her side armed with vases, boxes of holders, ribbons

All the others are suddenly reduced to gaping in silence

Lettice Oh, someone's been rather naughty here. I do have priority, you know. What absolute chaos! Never mind (*She calmly moves all the other things off the table and puts hers back on*)

The others seem mesmerized, unable to prevent Lettice

Carrie (*the first to recover*) Watch it! I don't want a thistle up my nostril!
Lettice Nostril yes but thistle no! It's a teazle.
Carrie Whatever it is, take it away from me.
Lettice (*to Joyce*) Ah, you look as if you ought to be in charge. Hello, you probably don't know me.
Joyce That's probably true. Do we have to spoil it now by meeting? To put it as plainly as I can: who are you?
Lettice Lettice.
Joyce And I'm bananas. Or I soon will be.

A Slight Misunderstanding

Lettice I've come to give a talk on flower arrangements without flowers.
Joyce How clever. But someone must have made a silly mistake. Hetty asked me to give a talk on wine-making. Where is Hetty?
Carrie (*roaring at the audience*) Hetty!
Joyce Isn't she here, Audrey?
Audrey Apparently not. I've never known her let people down like this. She's always been so dependable.
Lettice Perhaps she has decided to change her image.
Carrie What does that mean? Do you even know her?
Lettice Does one even know oneself?
Joyce In your case I rather doubt if it's worth any effort.
Lettice At least I have a letter from her.
Joyce Can I see it, please? (*She takes it*) Oh, yes, that's her writing. My God, she's giving you a fee and expenses!
Lettice Of course. I am a professional demonstrator. (*She takes her letter back before the others can read it*)
Carrie I thought the idea was to have my jumble this afternoon.
Joyce I thought we were to give some of our keener amateurs the chance to show what they can do. We all feel we could do as well as some of these so-called professionals. I was to be first, today. Then next time, Effie was to talk on cookery. After that—(*she looks round and sees Irma's squashed string*)—ah, yes, Irma was to demonstrate lampshades.
Irma I am certain Hetty asked me to do it today.
Effie I'm certain she fixed today for me.
Audrey She told me there was a play on.
Lettice Something smells funny, doesn't it?
Carrie No-one is better equipped than you to find out. Come on, Joyce, you're on the committee. What are we going to do?
Joyce (*to the audience*) Oh dear, please can you be patient for a moment while we try to reach a decision?
Carrie First, what are we going to do about Snitchabelle here?
Joyce I suppose we are obliged to pay her fee anyway.
Lettice Insults don't bother me but I insist that you should honour your obligations.
Irma Give her the money and get rid of her.
Lettice I always believe in being constructive.
Irma (*holding up a squashed lampshade*) You'd better have a go at this then.

Lettice You don't need to pay me for nothing. I'm still prepared, even in the appalling circumstances, to give a short talk. Still, I suggest, the amateurs should each have a chance as well.

Effie What chance?

Lettice Say five minutes each. Like a kind of TV talent contest. The audience can be asked to applaud or vote at the end. Then the winner can be awarded the chance to give a full talk at the next meeting.

Joyce I must admit, that's not a bad idea. Five minutes each. We need someone impartial. Audrey! You can be the timekeeper and referee.

Audrey Fair enough.

Joyce And as we wanted to see how we compare with the professionals, Lettice here is also in the contest. She can speak last —and only for the same time.

Carrie Lovely! Good for all of you. High jinks all round. What about my jumble?

Joyce You can have it very quickly afterwards. It won't take long if anyone's interested.

Carrie Of course they are! (*She helps herself to a chair and sits at the side of the stage*)

Joyce Effie first then.

Effie If I am to have the responsibility of going first, I must have space.

Joyce Quite right. Let's clear the decks for her.

Lettice, Joyce and Irma clear the table and Effie places her trays there. She stands in position for her talk while the others arrange chairs and sit down to listen

Effie I don't know where to begin. I wasn't prepared for only five minutes. I feel like a Channel swimmer who's fallen in a puddle.

Joyce It's the same for all of us. Are you ready, Audrey?

Audrey Yes.

Joyce Effie's five minutes begin—now!

Effie Ah, um . . .

Joyce Come on. We're not expecting an impression of Marlon Brando. What are you talking about?

Effie Cookery. Unusual recipes. Little tips and hints.

Irma Who does she think she is—Cranny Faddock?

A Slight Misunderstanding 9

Carrie No no, she's the Golloping Garmet.
Joyce Ladies! Be fair. Come on, Effie.
Effie It *was* Fanny Craddock who said that only someone with the soul of a rabbit enjoys lettuce as it is usually served. Dressing a salad is the subject for a complete talk on its own. So I'm not going to do that. I was going to talk about aspic jelly but . . .
Carrie I put my foot in it.
Effie Well, it is good for glazing things—galantine and cold meat, pâtès and chicken pieces. What's left over can be chopped up like that was and arranged around a foot—food—food!—as a decoration. Appearances are so important, aren't they? (*She becomes fascinated by Lettice, who is staring at her, and forgets what she was going to say*) Ah, um . . .
Joyce Appearances, appearances.
Effie That's what put me off. Isn't it nice when you cut a cherry cake and see all those jolly cherries evenly spaced out, not in a gooey blob at the bottom. How do you stop cherries from sinking? Shake them round in a sieve with some flour. When they're well coated you can fold them in the mixture.
Irma I like them in a gooey blob.
Effie (*to Irma*) I was also going to suggest what you could do with your leftovers. Ah, I have some notes here on unusual recipes.
Joyce Black mark. She's resorted to notes.
Effie French Yorkshire pudding is very good. Herring soup with raspberry jelly is not. I tried it. In sauces which have yolk of egg as the main ingredient, they must never be allowed to boil. If they do, the elements become disunited.
Irma Fancy!
Effie That's right. They curdle. Ah, um . . .
Joyce You've brought a lot of stuff with you, Effie. Aren't you going to make something? Has she any time left, Audrey?
Audrey Believe it or not, about three minutes.
Effie There is a little flummery that is such fun for the kiddywinks—Banana Candlesticks. You put some pineapple rings on a plate like this. Theh you find some straight bananas. (*She has problems with this*) Skin them. Cut some lengths to fit in the pineapple centres like candles. (*They will not stand up*) Really, before you fix them you should roll them in jam and chopped

nuts. (*She gets in a mess*) Of course if you don't like nuts, just —stick—to the jam. There must be some sort of jam you like . . . When you have them upright on the pineapple rings (*she at last gets one to stand up*) put a bit of glacé cherry on the top like a flame. A curved thin strip of angelica stuck in the side of the banana looks like the candlestick handle. (*she tries to do it with a straight piece of angelica which flicks away from her fingers as she tries to curve it and she knocks the banana over*) To soften angelica so you *can* fix it in place, you do have to put it in boiling water for a few minutes—but I don't have any with me. When the candlesticks are properly finished they do look really jolly.

Joyce I'm sure they do.
Effie It feels as if my time is up.
Audrey Just about.
Joyce Thank you very much, Effie.

Effie goes to a chair, sits on it with her back to the others and tries to clean her jammy hands on tissues

Effie I've failed. It wasn't fair. I'm not suited for the rat race.
Joyce It was a brave attempt, Effie, never mind.
Effie Never mind? Why don't you try it? See how you get on.
Joyce Very well, I will, although in the time available I can only try to awaken an interest in the subject.
Carrie See if you can awaken me then.

Carrie does at least help Joyce clear the table and put the wine and the wine-making equipment in place. Carrie sits again

Joyce Thanks. Right.
Audrey Are you ready? Go!
Joyce Making your own wine at home. Wine is not just the living blood of the grape. It can be made from the prepared and fermented juice of many kinds of fruit and vegetable. To be honest, wine is both good and bad. It's good if you enjoy it, if it complements your food, if it softens the outlines of a hard day. It can be bad if—like any drink and other things as well—it is taken in excess.
Carrie That's right. My old man fell over the tortoise and broke his leg.
Irma Poor tortoise.

A Slight Misunderstanding 11

Carrie No no, it was my old man's leg.
Joyce That's nothing. My Great Uncle Herbert inflated like an airship and drifted out of the french windows. He suffered from contusions and confusion before we could recapture him. And if fermentation continues, when wine is only supposed to be maturing, the bottles can blow up like small bombs. We have a number of corks embedded in our larder ceiling. Also squeaky and guggly noises can cause marital problems. It is all too easy to accuse one's husband of them when he is entirely innocent. However, there are very few worthwhile things that do not have minor drawbacks.
Carrie How terribly terribly true! Roll on jumble time.
Joyce Wine-making is easy enough. The most important ingredient is patience. You do need equipment like this. Containers, pails, jars, bottles and many little items from bored bungs to corking tools. You need ingredients—"must", yeast and tablets and things. The yeast is for fermentation. Without fermentation there is no alcohol. Without alcohol it is not wine. You have to do racking, fining and filtering to get rid of the lees and gunge. Then you have to wait because wine is really sickening until it is matured . . . Now, must is made by boiling water and sugar with a preparation of (*she reels off the following list at high speed, with occasional emphasis of odder ones*) apple, apricot, aubergine, balm, banana, barley, beet sugar, beetroot, bilberry, birch sap, blackberry, black currant, broad bean, broom, burdock, burnet, cabbage, canned fruit, carnation, celery, chamomile, cherry, clover, colt's foot, caramel, cowslip, cranberry, damson, dandelion, dewberry, elderberry, fennel, fig, ginger, golden rod, gooseberry, gorse, grapefruit, greengage, guava, hawthorn berry, honeysuckle, kohl rabi, lavender, lemon, lemon thyme, lime, loganberry, loquat, lovage, mahonia, malt, marigold, meadow sweet, medlar, melomel, mint, mulberry, nectarine, nettle, oak leaf, onion, orange, pansy, parsley, parsnip, passion fruit, paw-paw, peach, peapod, pear, pineapple, plum, potato, primrose, prune, pumpkin, quince, raisin, raspberry, red currant, rhubarb, rice, rose hip, rosemary, rose petal, rowanberry, sarsaparilla, sloe, strawberry, sultana, tangerine, tea, tomato, turnip, vanilla, wallflower, walnut leaf, wheat, woodruff and yarrow—and many blends of lots of these! In fact, there is a fair amount of choice

and wine-making can be quite a busy hobby. Now I have a small selection of my own wines here. It is obviously impossible to hand them round to everybody. So I thought I'd try them out on two people. One would know a bit about home-made wine. The other would know very little. Carrie, you make it, don't you? Are you an expert?

Carrie I'm prepared to stick my neck out.

Joyce That's very sporting of you. Now who could do with cheering up? Effie?

Effie Not likely.

Joyce Irma. Do you know anything about home-made wine?

Irma I can't say I do.

Joyce This is your big chance then. Come on. Stand and face the audience both of you.

Irma I'm not at all sure . . .

Carrie Oh, come on. What have you got to lose apart from your innards?

Carrie and Irma take their places with Joyce who tips out some wine into two glasses for them

Carrie Steady there, Joyce. She's not used to it, remember.

Joyce What's that one, Carrie?

Carrie Orange. Just a little bit like sherry. Not bad. Too dry for her I should think.

Irma Dry! It's bitter.

Joyce A taste for drier wines is something you have to cultivate.

Carrie A touch of tansy?

Joyce No.

Carrie A little caramel?

Joyce No. (*She pours from another bottle*) This is medium sweet, Irma. You should like that better.

Carrie (*drinking*) Blackberry.

Irma Ooh, yes. That's good.

Joyce (*pouring again*) Here you go.

Carrie It's—er—ah, yes, carrot?

Joyce Carrot it is.

Irma It might be all right for an alcoholic donkey but not for me.

Joyce (*pouring*) What about this then?

Carrie That is very smooth. But it's cheating for a home-made wine snob like me.

A Slight Misunderstanding

Irma It tastes like real wine to me.
Joyce If you mean it is made from grape juice, you are correct. Now be honest. What did you think? Carrie?
Carrie Eight out of ten. The orange was best.
Irma I'm not sure. Let's try that blackberry again. (*She helps herself to a large measure*)
Joyce Careful, Irma. That one's fortified and more than usual. My cat pushed my elbow when I was adding some brandy. She wanted her fishies.
Irma Yes, I think I like it. I must make absolutely sure. (*She helps herself again*)
Joyce No, Irma, please. You haven't given your talk yet. (*She holds the bottle behind her*)
Irma Yes, I do like it. I would be interested in how to make that. (*She looks for the bottle*)
Joyce There you are, ladies, approval from an expert and a testimonial from a beginner.
Carrie (*almost forcibly taking Irma back to her chair*) Come on now. Sit down there, like a good girl.
Joyce How was that for timing, Audrey?
Audrey You were a little over.
Carrie Wow, suddenly I don't think I feel very well—like I've swallowed a cannonball. Does home-made wine have any effect on you, Joyce?
Joyce I really don't know. It's probably worse if you mix them.
Carrie You mixed them. Why don't you know?
Joyce Oh, I never drink it myself. I just enjoy making it.
Carrie Great!

Joyce tidies up her things and moves out of the way

Lettice I think that was disgraceful. Little better than an orgy.
Irma An orgy? Where?
Joyce Irma! Pull yourself together. I suggest you do your piece next before the wine really gets to you.
Irma I must say, I feel ready for anything. (*A radiant smile transforms her face. She gets her box and stands behind the table*) Let's shoot, Aud!
Audrey All right.
Irma I must be serious. (*She resumes her normal expression of*

misery) Lampshades are dull. The opposite of what they should be. That is, if they're made of plastic, parchment, paper, raffia and all the usual old materials, they're dull. If they're made of string they are not. They are not dull. They are sparkling. (*She holds up the squashed ones*) Or at least they were sparkling. Perhaps some of you saw them before the elephant stampede. The amazing, astonishing fact is how easy it is to make them with string like this. I'll show you. First you blow up a balloon. I bet you would never have thought of that! Making lampshades by blowing up a balloon. (*She blows up a balloon with some difficulty*)

Carrie Just relax, Irma, you're not being breathalyzed.

Effie (*nervously*) That balloon is fast becoming a deadly weapon.

Irma is disconcerted, lets it go and it propels itself round fitfully

Lettice Really!

Irma Look what you made me do! It's gone. I'll have to try again. (*She blows up another balloon*)

Lettice The suspense is killing me.

Effie You keep your . . . Mind your own business.

Irma There. Could someone kindly help me? (*She holds the neck of the balloon*)

Joyce deftly ties it up for her

Thanks, Joyce. Now for the string. (*She winds string round and round the balloon to make a kind of abstract lace pattern and tucks in the end*) See? I'll show you. (*She takes it round to those on stage*) It is really simple.

When Irma gets near Lettice, the balloon bursts. Could Lettice have pricked it?

Effie Oh, my nerves!

Irma How did that happen? (*She glares at Lettice then goes back to her place*) This doesn't seem to be my lucky day. Next you would normally paste the string with a good stiff size. Let it get really hard and *then* deflate your balloon—and you're left with a lampshade.

Carrie How do you get the bulb in?

Irma With scissors. I mean, you have to cut a hole in the top to fit the holder. Then you have to cut a larger hole in the bottom. That's for planting the bulb so it can bloom with light. And if

A Slight Misunderstanding

you paint the string it can be any colour you like. I have nothing more to say. (*She goes to her chair and sits down just in time before she falls*)

Audrey That was well under time.

Lettice It was quite long enough. Now it is my turn. (*She moves Irma's box out of the way and spreads all her materials on the table before her*)

Joyce Time her, Audrey.

Audrey Right. Starting now!

Lettice The professional prepares a talk with care. I believe in starting with a definition. For instance, if I had been talking about recipes I should have begun with this: "Cookery is the art of preparing and presenting food of all sorts for human consumption, of converting the raw materials into a digestible and pleasing condition, for the satisfaction of the appetite and the delight of the palate."

Effie What if you don't like all sorts?

Lettice An authentic gastronome would.

Irma I don't like gnomes. There's no such thing as a female gnome. Didn't you know that?

Audrey You're wasting time talking about cookery.

Lettice I think it is relevant. If I had been talking about wine...

Audrey You're still wasting time. You're just knocking at the others.

Lettice Very well. Flower arranging is the centuries old art of composing flowers, foliage and fruit-bearing branches in a vessel for the decoration of a room. Without flowers it is even more of an art. The ancient Japanese established the basic principles. A tall spray represents heaven, the low one is earth and in between is poor old mankind. They introduced the idea of disturbed symmetry. They also arranged things differently when it was to be viewed from the front only—what they called a hanging picture—or from all round. Unhappily, I do not have time for subtleties. I cannot delve, for example, into the Japanese style of autumnal arrangements suggesting the singing of insects.

Carrie That's something.

Lettice By such finer things of life we can demonstrate that civilization really has a meaning. Yet it is not necessary for such ornamentation to be expensive. That is why I am advocating arrangements without flowers. "The Flower that once has blown for ever dies." The pursuit of what is rather quaintly called husbandry is a matter of some seriousness. As Lady Macbeth said, before she finally went round the twist, "There's husbandry in heaven." And cut flowers can be hellishly expensive. Very well then. The answer is this—(*she holds up a teazle*)—this—(*she holds up a leafy branch*)—and this! (*She holds up some pampas grass*) And maybe one or two other things as well. And there is endless guile in their juxtaposition. Do you follow me?

Irma No.

Lettice Well, persevere.

Irma I like flowers.

Lettice Flowers in arrangement never recovered from those old Dutch paintings. They look all right in oils perhaps. But really! Snails slithering all over the place. Birds' nests full of droppings. Insects everywhere. Arrangements work perfectly well without earwigs. Where was I? Disturbed symmetry is not enough. You also need contrast. Contrast is necessary to give vitality. You need soft contrasted with hard, sharp with rounded, sweet with sour, fat with thin, colour with monotone and the prickly—(*she holds up a teazle*)—with—(*she holds up a pampas grass*)—the tickly. Such contrasts make a world of difference to cooking and art as well as flower arrangements—and, I have no doubt, to married life as well. Would it be an exaggeration to say that civilization is virtually meaningless without the more agreeable polarities?

Carrie I need time to think about that before I answer. Or do I?

Lettice Going on from all this theorizing, where are we? In practice, we need a vessel, a means of holding sprays in place in the vessel and of course the things themselves that are held in place in the vessel by such means.

Joyce I don't believe it.

Carrie It's a load of codswallop. I think she's having us on.

Lettice Come, come, woman, is professionalism so hard to appreciate?

Carrie Don't you "woman" me, you gas-propelled beak!

Lettice Isn't it worth effort to understand concepts that would otherwise remain beyond your grasp?

A Slight Misunderstanding 17

Carrie Not if they're your concepts. You haven't got an idea in you that would stimulate a louse.
Lettice I have no wish to stimulate a louse.
Audrey I agree with Carrie. I refuse to call on the audience to declare what they think. The contest couldn't be taken seriously, could it, Joyce?
Joyce Pity. I thought my five minutes went rather well.
Audrey It's up to Hetty to sort it all out.
Lettice (*sharply*) You don't seem to have got the message yet. Let me read you all a part of Hetty's letter. "Everyone in the guild is perfectly happy to take what I do for granted. I have asked again and again for someone else to organize the talks. People are constantly complaining about my speakers but they won't take it on themselves. P.S. Tell them to remember there is a dog training session in the hall at six o'clock."
Carrie Oh, I've got it. I know who you are!
Joyce Who?
Effie I don't understand why Hetty should put all that in a letter to you. Why doesn't she tell us herself?
Carrie That would be telling.
Lettice (*to Effie*) She said she did. No-one listened.
Irma (*advancing on Lettice unsteadily*) Where is she then? Has she run away to Timbuctoo? I don't like you. What's it to do with you at all? When I was making my lampshade you bust my balloon, didn't you? You thought I didn't realize because I'd had alco—alcoholly—alcoll—alcolic—an alc—oh, a blackberry juice.
Lettice (*retreating*) Stay away from me. You are hopelessly inebriated. Stop.
Irma No. Just you stop. It's up to you to stop it.
Lettice Stop what?
Irma Stop pointing at me.
Lettice Pointing? What's pointing?
Irma Your n-o-s-e. Your nose! That! (*She gets hold of it*)
Lettice Ouch! Let go! (*It sounds like "Led do!"*)

The nose comes away in Irma's hand

Irma What have I done? (*She drops it in horror*)
Joyce I do believe you have found Hetty for us.

Joyce marches up to Lettice and uncovers Hetty further, the glasses first then the hat. They all stand and stare at Hetty, really an attractive, bright person who speaks normally enough

Carrie I was right. What was the idea, Hetty? I never thought you had a sense of humour like that.

Joyce I'm not at all sure it was a practical joke. She wanted to make fools of us, which she did.

Hetty Not really, Joyce. It must seem rather silly now and I didn't really mean to be vindictive. I thought of it as a sort of protest.

Joyce Well, finally, I do get the point. As it happens, I am the only one of the committee here today. Still, I can assure you, we will see our way to accepting your resignation.

Hetty Oh, but please, Joyce, I didn't mean to offend you personally. I don't want to leave the guild. I have so many friends here.

Carrie Yes, take it easy, Joyce. She is right, you know. We haven't been fair to her.

Joyce (*after a pause*) Yes! Of course, Hetty. We really owe *you* an apology. We have taken you for granted. We haven't been nearly appreciative enough.

Irma That's all very well. I'm not sure I'll recover from this in a hurry. (*But she does. She suddenly bursts out laughing*)

Effie Nor me. What about my aspic?

Irma And my balloon! (*She laughs again*)

Carrie (*laughing*) One thing's for sure, we've never had a meeting like this before!

Hetty (*to the audience*) After all, it was only a slight misunderstanding.

Audrey quickly joins the others on stage as they line up and formally make their salutation to the audience. In this way they signify that the play has come to the very end and

the CURTAIN *falls*

FURNITURE AND PROPERTY LIST

On stage: Small, plain trestle table
5 stacking chairs in one pile

Off stage: Piles of typical jumble including bowler hat and rolled umbrella, weird toys, fantastic objects **(Carrie)**
Cardboard box with uninflated balloons, string, paste, paintbrush, 2 completed and brightly coloured string lampshades, scissors **(Irma)**
Eggs, flour, sugar, seasoning, milk, heap of chopped jelly on tray, load of pineapple rings, bananas, jam, chopped nuts, glace cherries, angelica strips, plate, bowl, whisk, spoon, timer **(Effie)**
Bottles of apparent home-made wines in box: orange, blackberry, carrot, grape juice, wine-making equipment, 2 glasses on tray **(Joyce)**
Teazles, pampas grass, branches of dried leaves, evergreen branches, bulrushes, reeds, grasses, etc., and various vases, ribbons, plant-holders, etc. **(Lettice)**

Personal: **Effie:** tissues
Lettice: letter
Audrey: watch

LIGHTING PLOT

Property fittings required: nil
A bare stage
To open: Houselights on
Cue 1   As **Carrie** climbs up on stage   (Page 1)
      Fade houselights—bring up general stage lighting to full

www.ingramcontent.com/pod-product-compliance
Ingram Content Group UK Ltd.
Pitfield, Milton Keynes, MK11 3LW, UK
UKHW021849210426
5322IPUK00022B/553